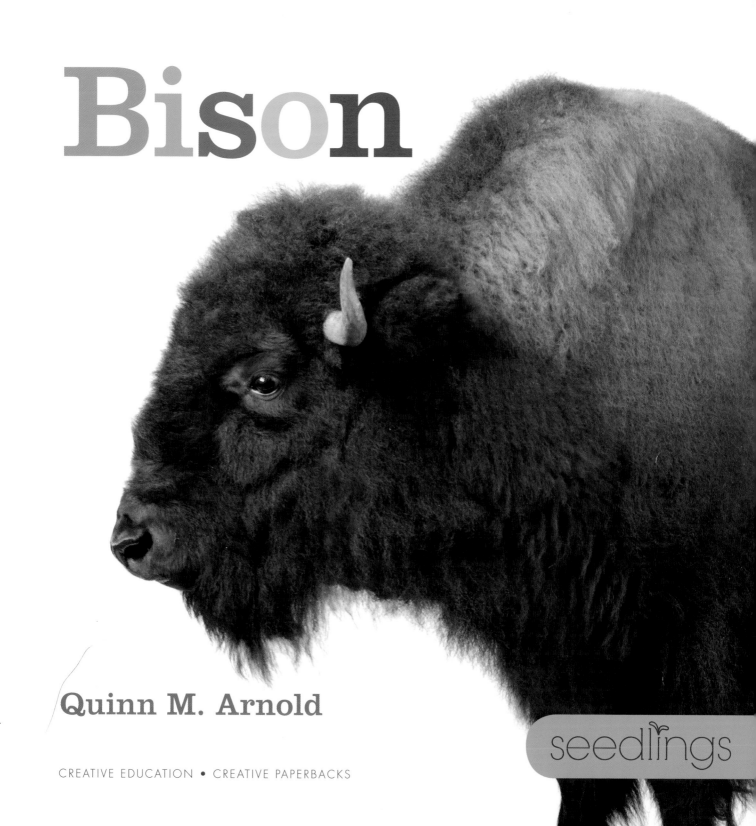

Bison

Quinn M. Arnold

CREATIVE EDUCATION • CREATIVE PAPERBACKS

seedlings

Published by Creative Education and Creative Paperbacks
P.O. Box 227, Mankato, Minnesota 56002
Creative Education and Creative Paperbacks
are imprints of The Creative Company
www.thecreativecompany.us

Design by Ellen Huber; production by Joe Kahnke
Art direction by Rita Marshall
Printed in the United States of America

Photographs by Alamy (Keith Crowley, Andrew Kandel),
Corbis (IMAGEMORE/Imagemore Co., Ltd.), Dreamstime
(Rinus Baak, Betty4240, Isselee, Lynnbellphoto, Madd, Msg-s,
Glenn Nagel, Uros Petrovic, Sherry Young, Abeselom Zerit),
Flickr (Brian Gratwicke), iStockphoto (Nancy Honeycutt,
JohanWelzenga, MarkD800), National Geographic Creative
(JOEL SARTORE), Shutterstock (Eric Isselee)

Library of Congress Cataloging-in-Publication Data
Arnold, Quinn M.
Bison / Quinn M. Arnold.
p. cm. — (Seedlings)
Includes bibliographical references and index.
Summary: A kindergarten-level introduction to bison,
covering their growth process, behaviors, the forests and
grasslands they call home, and such defining features as their
shaggy fur.
ISBN 978-1-60818-795-9 (hardcover)
ISBN 978-1-62832-348-1 (pbk)
ISBN 978-1-56660-842-8 (eBook)
1. American bison—Juvenile literature.
QL737.U53 A765 2016
599.64/3—dc23   2015041992
CCSS: RI.K.1, 2, 3, 4, 5, 6, 7;
RI.1.1, 2, 3, 4, 5, 6, 7; RF.K.1, 3; RF.1.1

First Edition HC 9 8 7 6 5 4 3 2 1
First Edition PBK 9 8 7 6 5 4 3 2 1

TABLE OF CONTENTS

Hello, bison!

Bison are the biggest land animals in North America.